D0310861

NORTHAMPTONSHIRE IN WINTER

BOB CADDICK

HALSGROVE

First published in Great Britain in 2010

Copyright © Bob Caddick 2010

All rights reserved. No part of this publication may be reproduced,
stored in a retrieval system, or transmitted in any form or by any
means without the prior permission of the copyright holder.

British Library Cataloguing-in-Publication Data
A CIP record for this title is available from the British Library

ISBN 978 0 85704 057 2

HALSGROVE
Halsgrove House,
Ryelands Industrial Estate,
Bagley Road, Wellington, Somerset TA21 9PZ
Tel: 01823 653777   Fax: 01823 216796
email: sales@halsgrove.com

Part of the Halsgrove group of companies
Information on all Halsgrove titles is available at: www.halsgrove.com

Printed and bound in by Grafiche Flaminia, Italy

FOREWORD

Is there a greater evocation of the winter season than Shakespeare's sonnet, simply called *Winter*, I wonder?

> *When icicles hang by the wall*
> *and Dick the shepherd blows his nail*
> *and Tom brings logs into the hall*
> *and milk comes frozen home in pail;*
> *When blood is nipt, and way be foul*
> *Then nightly sings the staring owl*
> *Tu-whoo!*
> *Tu-whit, tu-whoo! A merry note*
> *While greasy Joan doth keel the pot*

I have tried to capture some of the scenes painted in the poem in my own photographs of the Northamptonshire countryside between Harvest time and Easter…when the casual visitor disappears and eventually only the true countryman or farmers are left to live in the bleak landscape. I have found the icicles and the frozen sheep, although no shepherds were to be seen! Stacks of logs sit waiting for a modern day Tom to bring them in to warm us on the fire…

Winter comes on subtly, by degree, from the last rays of warming sun on stubble wheat fields to the gradual colouring of the leaves in the hedgerows. In October, the townsfolk of Oundle encourage visitors to their area with their annual World Conker Championships, celebrating the glorious sight of glossy chestnuts falling on village greens everywhere in the county. Town dwellers often miss these seasonal changes as their environment is constantly warmed and lit artificially – only to get a shock when winter hits them hard with freezing rains and snows, frosts that freeze the locks in the car door and "blood is nipt" by the freezing air. Then the complaints about the "awful weather" start…

To be outdoors in these wintry conditions is a privilege for a landscape photographer like me… on sunny bright days the air is crystal clear and the light brilliant in its intensity. And on overcast, grey days the landscape takes on a simple monochrome appearance with shapes reduced to silhouettes or smudges against the sky.

Our wildlife has learned to live with the changes that winter brings, sensibly hibernating like hedgehogs, or becoming more active like the thousands of small birds that are constantly foraging for food…taking the gleanings from the now deserted harvest fields or remainders of long picked sprouts or turnips

We celebrate the darkest days after the solstice with lights and festivals, and once again the Christmas trees are carried home or placed in our town centres and villagers gather for the switching on of their lights. But this in turn, signifies the beginning of the end of winter, soon snowdrops will push their noses though the frozen ground and daffodils will brave the chilly air. Winter can still have a sting in its tail though, as shown in my photograph of Castle Ashby house one Easter Sunday, when the daffodils were blooming but suddenly found themselves up to their trumpets in snow.

At last the sun will win its annual battle with the north wind and gets us to remove our top coats and layers; spring is here and summer is waiting in the wings full of showy splendour…but winter will be back to test us all again next year.

Bob Caddick

Castle Ashby Harvest
Storm clouds gather as all is "safely gathered in" near Grendon. The oncoming winter will change the landscape dramatically as frost and snow break down the ground into a surface suitable for sowing next spring.

Opposite:

Ready for Harvest Burton Latimer's wheatfields burst with grain ready for the coming harvest. Thousands of tonnes of local wheat are used each year by Weetabix who have a major production unit at Burton Latimer.

Ancient Oak at Rockingham
The first signs of fall are showing in this ancient oak at the top of Rockingham Hill, near Corby. The steep hill at Rockingham provides a view over at least three counties and was a natural choice for Henry the Eighth's great fortress on the top of the escarpment. Charles Dickens was a regular visitor to Rockingham and I like to think that he may have taken a stroll around the trunk of this ancient tree!

Pasture Land at Eyebrook
A dairy herd grazes quietly by the Uppingham Road from Rockingham, making the most of fresh grass before they will have to rely on hay and silage.

6

Potato Harvest
Farmers work hard throughout the autumn gathering and storing crops for the winter. This farm near Rushden, still uses hand pulling and sack filling methods instead of the more automated way, which is better suited to the vast fields of East Anglia. Their customers appreciate the more "natural" methods when they buy from the farm gate.

World Conker Championship

October means the annual "World Conker Championships" at Ashton village, near Oundle where the conkers are all hand-picked and selected to ensure fair play. Starting out as an alternative to a rained off fishing trip, Ashton's conker championships have become a national institution.

Opposite:
Conkers at Ashton

Great crowds come to Ashton each year to see hundreds of competitors take part in the major fund raising event, where many contestants wear fancy dress and protection from flying chestnuts.

King Conker

King Conker, aka David Jakins, makes an imposing figure at the championships in Ashton.

Elton
Bright sunshine illuminates this vista of trees at Elton Hall on the Cambridgeshire border.

Newton Bromswold

As the days grow cooler, sheep seek out shelter from winter winds. This tree-sheltered hollow at Newton Bromswold is a perfect place to keep warm. Newton Bromswold's village pub, The White Swan, was mentioned in one of H. E. Bates' novels.

Bare Earth at Newton Bromswold
With the harvest gathered in the fields will lie dormant until winter has passed and fresh crops can be planted.

Fields near Easton Maudit

Easton Maudit hamlet lies near to the Compton estates at Castle Ashby, and must be one of the smallest settlements in the county. Originally known simply as Easton, the Maudit family purchased the land and village in 1131.

Near Yardley Hastings
Enjoying what may be the last of the autumn sunshine, this flock of sheep make a peaceful pastoral scene on the road to Yardley Hastings.
Much of Northamptonshire's historic wealth has derived from the wool and leather industries.

Winter Fuel

Shakespeare's Tom would have been familiar with a site like this as he was sent to carry logs into the hall to keep his master warm during the winter season. These logs at Sywell Country Park will probably serve the same purpose in the twenty-first century as they would have in the fifteenth!

Cosgrove Bridge
One of the few individually designed bridges on the Grand
Union Canal, this bridge at Cosgrove is a lovely sight on
a winter's walk along the towpath.

Cosgrove Moorings
Moored safely for the winter, these canal boats and
cruisers will manage to avoid the worst of the weather
thanks to the sheltering trees at Cosgrove.

Harringworth
A rare sight as a passenger train crosses the mighty viaduct at Harringworth, reflected in the wetlands of the Welland Valley below.

Fotheringhay Church Approach

A golden archway lines the walk to the entrance of the church at Fotheringhay as leaves have their final flush of colour before falling.
Fotheringhay Castle was the scene of Mary, Queen of Scots' imprisonment and execution in 1587.
Fotheringhay is also notorious as the birthplace of King Richard III in 1432.

Northampton Guild Hall
Northampton's Gothic County Council headquarters, the Guild Hall, glitters in October sunlight. Designed by Edward Godwin and built in 1861, the Guild Hall contains a Great Hall decorated with portraits of many of the famous men associated with the town. The lobby contains a memorial to Spencer Perceval, who was the MP for Northampton and had the rather unlucky distinction of being the only British Prime Minister to have been assassinated!

Burton Latimer Wind Farm
Late November sunshine adds a golden glow to the blades of the turbines at Burton Latimer.
Personally, I love the look of the giant propellers as they gently rotate in the wind.

Ashby St Ledgers Gateway
This famous village, the scene of much of the planning of the Gunpowder Plot of 1605, is a fine example of Northamptonshire ironstone houses and buildings. The winter sunshine mellows the stone to a golden glow shortly after Hallowe'en.

Gunpowder Plot Room at Ashby St Ledgers
The long November shadows reach across the path to the very room where the Gunpowder Plot was hatched. Now in a poor state of repair, this half-timbered gate house stands in silent witness in the pretty village of Ashby St Ledgers, near Daventry.

Dewy Teasels
Heavy dew and morning mists mark the turning of the seasons as winter tightens its grip on the countryside.
These teasel heads draped in bejewelled cobwebs foretell a chilly day ahead.

Misty Cygnets

Still in immature plumage, this cygnet prepares to spend the winter hiding amongst the reed beds at Stanwick Lakes.
The morning air was chilled with icy mist as I captured this scene, and the wildfowl swam silently away into the haze just after
this shot was taken. Stanwick Lakes have been developed over the last few years, following the extraction of sand and gravel,
into a major leisure facility for the county, with miles of nature trails and bird watching facilities.

Fotheringhay Church

Mid-November and a melancholic stillness descends on Fotheringhay in the fading afternoon light. Mary, Queen of Scots, may have gazed out at this view often during her exile in the village.

Stanwick Lakes Flood

More typical of an English winter than the deep snow we would all like to imagine, heavy rain brings flooding to the play areas at Stanwick Lakes.

Easton Maudit Church
The first snow of winter sprinkles the fields near Easton Maudit with a light covering. The impressive spire of the village church in the background, marks the resting place of famous actor, Derek Nimmo, and was a regular place of worship for many other great figures including Dr Johnson and David Garrick.

Opposite:
Bullrushes
Reed mace at Stanwick Lakes provides much needed winter food for the flocks of small birds that winter amongst them.

Fawsley Hall Frost
A rapidly setting winter sun leaves behind a gin clear sky which will bring frost to Fawsley and its ancient church.

Opposite:
Fawsley Hall
Late sun near Christmas turns Fawsley's walls into an enchanting place in the shade of the old cedar trees. A great Elizabethan manor house, Fawsley Hall is now a luxurious hotel and restaurant – a far cry from its historic association with King Charles and the Battle at Naseby.

Thrapston Sheep
No shelter for these sheep near Thrapston as the sun disappears into thick snow-laden clouds, although lambing will begin in earnest in a few weeks time.

Chicheley College

Chicheley in Higham Ferrers was once one of England's finest colleges, but little now remains other than some perimeter walls and building outlines in the lawns. Founded by Henry Chichele, who was born in the town and became Archbishop of Canterbury, both Henry V and the Pope approved its construction. Only a century or so later, the college was "surrendered" to Henry VIII who dissolved it as a seat of learning. This rose was determined to bloom until the last rays of sun and warmth had left the sky, it seemed.

Stanwick Swans
Birds and other wildlife have the lakes to themselves as Christmas approaches and the walkers and joggers have other activities to pursue.

Stanwick Sunset

When the sun disappears in a fiery ball, leaving only a red glow in the sky, it is easy to understand how primitive people worried about it ever coming back again! We seem to have the same concerns every summer…

Stanwick Signpost

Remembrance Day poppies still lie at this memorial in the centre of Stanwick village. One of the old customs in Stanwick was to allow the young people of the village to "jangle" the bells of St Lawrence's church every Shrove Tuesday, but this has long been discontinued. Perhaps it is time to start again?

Naseby Battlefield
A menacing sky covers the site of the decisive battle of the English Civil War – a sky like this means more winter storms are on their way.

Carrying Christmas tree Home
What could be nicer than bringing home the tree from a nursery in the beautiful village of Upper Dean?

Singing Santa
Higham Ferrers Sparkle – here Santa is leading the Carol singing.

Higham Sparkle
This annual event draws massive crowds to the Market Square of Higham Ferrers to sing Christmas carols
and to see the switching on of the Christmas lights.

Christmas Trees
There is nothing to compare with the fragrance of a real Christmas tree in the house during the holidays.
This selection was on sale at Fineshade Woods Country Park near Corby.

Holly and Berries

What would Christmas be without holly berries? Their colour cheers us and they also provide food for the wild birds in the depth of winter. In Christian folklore the prickly leaves of Christmas holly trees came to be associated with Jesus' crown of thorns, while their berries represented the drops of blood shed for humanity's salvation. This symbolism can be found, for example, in the Christmas carol, *The Holly and The Ivy*. Christian folklore also identified Christmas holly wood as the wood used to build Jesus' holy cross. In fact, some scholars think that the word, "holly" is simply a corruption of "holy", although that may be a little over simplified.

MG Santa

Higham Ferrer's Sparkle event was graced by a rather modern Santa – it seems that a sleigh wasn't quite fast enough for the old boy, so an MG sports car was pressed into service!

Guildhall and Tree
Northampton town's imposing Guild Hall in festive mode with a beautifully lit tree in the weeks before Christmas.

December Evening Light
The sun has left the sky to an afterglow and this wonderful tree stands out in the gathering gloom of the landscape near Deenethorpe, a site of USAAF activity during the Second World War.

Winter Sunset at Fineshade Woods
The last glimmers of light and it is only mid afternoon, almost the shortest day at Fineshade Woods, near Corby.
Fineshade is managed by the Forestry Commission and has become popular with walkers and bird watchers who
come to view the growing flock of Red Kites that are seen regularly in the area.

Blue Bags
They are a common enough site on arable farms, but these blue bags provide a brilliant dash of colour to an otherwise monochrome landscape near Risely on the Bedfordshire border.

Woodland near Dean

Although seemingly empty this hedgerow was filled with the sound of birds foraging for food in this tiny village on the way to Bedfordshire. Famed as the setting of H. E. Bates' novel, *The Darling Buds of May*, Upper and Lower Dean are typical of many settlements on the Northamptonshire/Bedfordshire border.

Snow December
Although much maligned by some, a 4x4 is often the only way around in wintry conditions, and certainly the only way to cross this snow field near Yielden, where a shooting party had gathered on a beautifully crisp day.

Steep Hill, Collyweston
This steep slope proved too challenging for many drivers, fearful of a long slide all the way to the bottom!

Duddington Village

Duddington is a pretty village off the main road to Peterborough and Stamford – a little haven of tranquillity!

Upper Dean House

Right on the border and just into Bedfordshire, Upper and Lower Dean contain some of the most imposing village properties in the area.

Drying Kilns near Barrowden
Once used in the steel making process called calcification, these drying kilns at Barrowden reminded me of the turrets of some ancient castle.
They now lie silent save for the constant calling of the crows that have built their nests amongst them.

Opposite:
Red Berries in Duddington
It's no coincidence that Santa Claus wears red and white – they look so good together!

Snowy Bales

Looking like giant iced buns, these hay bales which provide much needed winter fodder glisten in the sun at Thrapston.

Farm Equipment
Long abandoned to winter's cold embrace, this equipment waits for warmer weather near Duddington.

Harringworth Archway
One of the viaducts' magnificent 82 arches makes a
great frame for the landscape beyond.

Harringworth from a Distance
Harringworth Viaduct is the longest masonry-built
railway crossing in the country.

Harringworth Viaduct in the Snow

Victorian engineering at its best, Harringworth viaduct looks even more imposing against the snowy background.
Built in the late 1880s with Williamson-Cliffe bricks, it must have been a wonder of the Victorian age.
Sadly, recent repairs have used a variety of brick types and have lent a "patchwork" appearance to the structure.

Winter's Fiery Skies
The old weather forecasters looked to the sky for their guidance – what would they have predicted for this dramatic scene near Oundle?

Christmas at Stanwick Lakes
A few days until Christmas and this solitary swan enjoys the peace of a quiet winter afternoon.

Hall Park Sledges
A slight slope and a smattering of snow are all it takes for kids to want their sledges out from storage!
The 30 or so acres of Hall Park in Rushden are a safe place to have fun.

Rushden Hall
Now the home of Rushden Town Council, Rushden Hall is one of the little town's oldest buildings and is an
exquisite Elizabethan manor house formerly owned by the Sartoris family.

Rushden War Memorial
Rushden's war memorial is an imposing monument and much loved by the residents of this town, once famous for its many shoe makers, including Sanders & Sanders who have made boots for the British Army for many years.

Rushden Hall Park Bench

On a summer afternoon this bench would resound to the music of the local silver band... but on a wintry December morning it remains unused!

Mears Ashby Skaters
An enterprising garden centre brought winter sports to the county with this open air skating rink,
which proved a great success with locals, young and old alike.

Fishing at Riverside Park
A hardy angler tries his luck at Riverside Park, although he needed to crack the ice before beginning to fish!

Upper Dean Church
A crisp morning in Upper Dean, the original setting for H. E. Bates' novel *The Darling Buds of May*.
H. E. Bates was born in nearby Rushden, and was one of the most prolific writers of the twentieth century.

Oundle Market after Christmas

The Christmas festivities are over and the search for bargains goes on at Oundle's street market in January. Oundle's claim to fame is the highly regarded public school which was founded in 1536 by Sir William Laxton, a resident of the town who became Lord Mayor of London.

Ashton Green

Surrounded by shady trees in summer, Ashton Green looks bare, save for the left over Christmas decorations in the trees outside The Chequered Skipper pub. The pub served as a shop and post office until the end of the war and was originally called The Three Horseshoes until the 1960s, when local landowner and resident Dame Miriam Rothchild renamed it. Dame Miriam was born in Ashton Wold in 1908 and lived there for most of her life. She was a world renowned zoologist, naturalist, academic and eccentric, often seen about the village in her mauve outfits and white wellingtons.

New Borns at Cottesbrooke
Mid-winter lambing often means that extra heat must be provided to ensure survival of weaker animals.
This ewe and her twins, just a few hours old, will soon be moved out to a cooler position.

Opposite:
Cottesbrooke
For sheep farmers, January means lambing is in full swing. And that means many sleepless nights for the shepherds.
Theses ewes at Cottesbrooke are all "ladies in waiting" with lambs due at any time.

Chelveston Snow drifts
Once the home of the USAAF 8th Bomb Group, Chelveston is now so quiet that
nothing evens disturbs the snow as it blows into mini drifts along the former runway.
The 305th BG, known as the "Can Do" group completed 480 missions, flying B-17
"Flying Fortresses". They lost 158 aircraft and 769 personnel died whilst carrying
out 9,231 aircraft sorties in the War from the now silent airfield.

Risely Mill
A favourite location, Risely Mill stands on the high ground where three counties,
Cambridgeshire, Bedfordshire and Northamptonshire meet.

Gretton War Memorial

A most impressive monument for such a small village, Gretton folk are rightly proud of their memorial on the village green. Built in 1925, the curved shape is an unusual feature for such a monument, but it fits in well with the other natural stone buildings of this hamlet. The village is also noted for having the tallest church tower in Northamptonshire, and the second-oldest running pub in the county, the Hatton Arms.

Opposite:
Ivy but no Holly

What a difference the addition of bright red holly berries would make to the dull green leaves of ivy growing wild near Newton Bromswold.

The Embankment Park, Wellingborough
Hot summer days see this park crowded with families, but not even a bird was singing on the day I photographed here as it was so cold.

Hot Food on the Embankment

Although there were no obvious customers for this catering van, he opened up "just in case" and sold me a coffee!

**A Bleak Landscape
near Rushden**
Winter can remove the colour
from the countryside, leaving
only the stark simplicity of line
and texture as here in the fields
on the A6 trunk road south
of Rushden.

Whitworth's Mill

A familiar sight to travellers on the A45 trunk road, Victoria Mill looks quite Dickensian in the snow. Founded in 1886 by the Whitworth family, the mill is still run by the firm today, producing fine flours for the bakery trade. In front of the mill there remains a jetty from the days when the river was used for transportation of goods to and from the mills.

Chelveston Church Snowdrops
This stunning annual display of snowdrops attracts scores of visitors to the little churchyard at Chelveston.

Snowdrops
Sales of January snowdrops "in the green" at the church porch raise useful funds for the upkeep of the old church at Chelveston.

Opposite:
Garden Crocus
I spotted this in my own garden in the same month, as a little patch of sunlight encouraged
an early crocus and an ambitious bee to get together with honey in mind!

Silver Birch

The crystal clear light of a bright winter day shows this silver birch tree in its true glory, with papery white peeling bark. Hundreds of people pass the tree on their daily trip to the railway station at Wellingborough – I hope at least some of them stop and enjoy the view!

The Embankment, Wellingborough

This flock of swans on the River Nene are well fed in summer when visitors provide bread in plenty, but it's a tougher time in January when the Embankment is often deserted for days on end.

Irthlingborough

With snow clouds massing behind the tower of St Peter's church at Irthlingborough, I think it has the look of an Italian campanile tower; originally this was a lantern tower standing on the high ground to show the safe passage across the marshy Nene Valley between Higham Ferrers and Irthlingborough.

Bailey Bridge
I love the repeating shapes of the structure of this Bailey Bridge, like a giant Meccano set!

Snowman at Stanwick

Snow can bring many problems in its wake, but these youngsters enjoy the day off school that a prolonged
snow fall has given them, and build a snowman at Stanwick Lakes Country Park.

Opposite:
Nene Bridge at Irthlingborough

Until relatively recently this bridge carried trunk traffic but now is a quiet place to fish and admire the view of the Nene.

Stanwick Morning
A little patch of blue brightens this overcast morning at Stanwick.

Bare Tree near Thrapston
Is it only me who appreciated the skeletal beauty of a bare tree? Trees look more dramatic
when their shape and form is not masked by leaves, in my opinion.

Titchmarsh Post Box
Brilliant sunshine after days of heavy
snowfall, and the colours take
on a new vibrancy in Titchmarsh.
The post box is positively glowing!

Farm Work
Snow may bring cities to a standstill,
but the work of a farm must carry
on, even if it means going to the job in the
back of a trailer as here near Titchmarsh.

High Street, Titchmarsh

Our street furniture could have been designed with winter snow in mind. What a good idea the Victorians had to paint them all red! It could have been so different though as *green* was adopted as the standard colour for the original early Victorian post boxes. Between 1866 and 1879 the hexagonal Penfold post box was chosen as the standard design for pillar boxes and it was during this period that red was first used as the standard colour. The first boxes to be painted red were in London in July 1874, although it would be nearly ten years before the rest of the country's boxes had been repainted.

The Wheatsheaf, Titchmarsh
The lovely old pub is feeling the benefit of early morning sunshine after an especially hard frost the night before. A slight thaw has started causing the roof to start dropping snow on to the pavements beneath. Once again our Northamptonshire Ironstone buildings are seen at their best in golden sunlight.

Chocolate Icicles
I spotted these hanging from a thatched cottage in Titchmarsh and they reminded me of
chocolate ice lollies – the house owner wondered what I found so fascinating!

Titchmarsh View
Just outside the village, the fields tell their own story of the prolonged heavy snowfall in January. The poet John Dryden lived here in childhood, and was possibly educated at the village school. More recently, the villagers campaigned to re-open their village shop and the opening ceremony was performed by TV gardener, Alan Titchmarsh.

Titchmarsh Church
The fine architecture of St Mary the Virgin church is enhanced by the early morning sunshine on the main road through Titchmarsh.

Yielden

Sitting on the border with Bedfordshire, Yielden takes on an alpine appearance the morning after a heavy snow shower.

Near Newton Bromswold
The empty fields reflect a pale winter sun near Newton Bromswold, named after the ancient forest that predated the village, Bruneswald Forest.

Near Rushden
Commuters on the busy A6 may not have a minute to enjoy this view as they hurry off to Bedford,
but I think this tree looks wonderful against the blue sky.

Nene at Ringstead

One of the coldest days of the winter and a light mist is rising from the River Nene at Ringstead. There was almost total silence as I took this photograph on a magical morning after a long walk across the snow-bound fields. The lakes at Ringstead are a popular fishing and shooting area.

Near Ringstead
The snow has the effect of highlighting the "hard" elements in a landscape, such as this little bridge over a Nene tributary near Ringstead.

Robin in snow

No tale of winter can be complete without a "Christmas card" robin! During winter our native garden birds are often joined by migratory Scandinavian robins, thus making their appearance at this time more common, and in fact many people are surprised when they learn that robins are resident the whole year! According to Christmas legend, a robin landed on the shoulder of Jesus and sang in order to relieve his suffering. The blood from Jesus' crown of thorns stained the little bird's chest, and from then on, all robins were red breasted. This one accompanied me for several hundred yards, bobbing in and out of the hedgerow as I walked, perhaps hoping for a morsel of breakfast!

Gulls at Brightwell Lake

The slightest noise was all it took to unsettle this flock of gulls on the frozen fishing lake at Brightwell, near Raunds.

Cold Ashby

What an appropriate name for a Northamptonshire hill village in winter. The village of Cold Ashby sits on the 200 metre (656 feet) contour line on some of the highest ground in the county. Perhaps the height of the village may have something to do with its name? Centuries ago the village would have been regularly isolated by winter snows, and perhaps with the climate changes we are now seeing it may be again in the future.

Cold Ashby Farm

This hillside farm catches the full force of the winter blizzards and seems to hunker down into the hillside
on one of the coldest days of the year, on the outskirts of Cold Ashby village.

Solo Skier

Looking more like Norway than Northamptonshire, this skier is enjoying the view from the top of one of the fairways at Cold Ashby Golf Club, where an enterprising management had converted the course into a ski run complete with lift and ski passes for a few days.

Skiing at Cold Ashby
Although not noted for its ski resorts, Northamptonshire became a winter sports resort temporarily
when Cold Ashby Golf Club converted the fairways into ski runs.

Horses at Barnwell
Although the sun is bringing some early warmth to the countryside,
these horses at Barnwell will still need their rugs for a few more weeks.

Barnwell Castle

Once home to the Duke and Duchess of Gloucester, and Princess Alice before that, the Barnwell Manor estate retains this fine ruin of a castle that was used as an armoury for the Royalist forces in the English Civil War. The last traces of snow can still be seen in the shade of the old walls.

Reflections near Polebrook
Saturated land after weeks of snow has turned a shallow depression
into a beautiful reflecting pond on the road from Polebrook.

Sunset over Polebrook Hill
As well as being a charming village, Polebrook was once home to the USAAF at their
base nearby. Famously commanded by American movie star, James Stewart, the old
runways still attract visitors to sign the memorial book. Clark Gable also served at
Polebrook during his service in the USAAF, so no doubt the local ladies were very
careful about their appearance when they went to the village shop in the 1940s!

Pitsford Sunset
After weeks of snow, the sun is beginning to melt the covering and gaps begin to appear on the reservoir's surface.
Opened in 1956 and now managed by Anglian Water, Pitsford covers 750 acres and also takes in Brixworth Country Park
and a nature reserve. Trout fishing from boats is a popular sport on the reservoir.

Ravensthorpe Reservoir

This small reservoir has an almost secret hidden feel, but it is still a popular place for fishermen and birdwatchers. Just 100 acres in size and sheltered by a gentle valley, Ravensthorpe is the oldest Anglian Water reservoir in the county, and was created in the Victorian era.

Trout Fishery at Pitsford
The trout fishing season is approaching and these dinghies are out of
the water for repairs and maintenance at Pitsford Water in February.

Ice on Pitsford Water
Clear water at last as the thaw continues at Pitsford,
allowing the birds back to their natural habitat.

Coton Manor Daffodils
Bright daffodils and snowdrops
illuminate a shady corner at
Coton Manor Gardens.

Coton Manor Hellebores
A bright February day and
the hellebores burst into bloom at
Coton Manor's shade garden.

Coton Manor

More commonly seen in the summer, Coton Manor is worth a visit in February when its famous Hellebore collection is at its best.

Kelmarsh
Farmers are out and about checking their land and livestock as February comes to a close here in Kelmarsh. The village is the home of the "Kelmarsh Tunnels", which are disused railway tunnels which now provide walks through the hillside, although they are unlit!. Both tunnels are 322 yards (294 m) long, and due to the small bore, were known as "the rat-holes" by train drivers.

Rushton Rainbow

The eternal symbol of hope and renewal, this rainbow appeared after days of torrential rain near Rushton and its imposing Elizabethan manor house, Rushton Hall, home of the Tresham family. The Treshams were influential Roman Catholics in the fifteenth century and later became involved with the Gunpowder Plot.

Chusan Palm at Castle Ashby

Whilst the less hardy plants must be protected in the glass houses at Castle Ashby this hardy Chusan Palm braves the snow and makes a stunning architectural feature in the winter garden at the castle. Castle Ashby was the summer home of the Compton family, whose main residence is at Compton Wynyates in Warwickshire. Now the home of Lord Compton, the Marquis of Northampton, the gardens are open regularly to the public.

Denford
Warm spring sunshine brings on the blossom and the riverside village of Denford is caught in the sunlight.

Finedon Rape Fields
The farmers watch the weather anxiously as sudden storms in March can ruin a field of canola, or rapeseed, like this near Finedon.

Terracotta Bridge
A favourite of the owner of Castle Ashby, the terracotta bridge is resplendent in March sunshine with the daffodils in full bloom.

Castle Ashby Camellia
This early flowering camellia fell victim to sudden snow
at Easter in the Castle Ashby Gardens.

Castle Ashby Easter Snow
Spring may have started to bring out the daffodils, but a
sudden snow fall overnight on Easter Sunday shows that
winter can still have a trick up its sleeve for the unwary.

Topiary at Castle Ashby
The topiary garden at Castle Ashby looks especially good on a snowy March day when the shapes of the yews can be better appreciated against the white background.

Castle Ashby Easter Egg Hunt

An Easter Egg hunt became more fun than usual when a sudden unpredicted snow fall covered the previously hidden eggs at Castle Ashby gardens – the children enjoyed it even more though!

Castle Ashby Creek

A watery scene in Castle Ashby gardens as the spring is delayed by late snowfall near the terracotta bridge.

Whitworth's Mill reflections
The sodden ground makes a mirror-like pool showing Whitworth's Mill across the Nene at Wellingborough.

Nene Moorings
Soon to be used by holiday cruisers, these moorings remain empty, as the spring advances along the Nene Valley, near Wellingborough.
Just across the river is the old jetty used by the original millers to transport goods around the country by water.

Tulips on the Embankment
Compare the scene in March to December's desolate view…
nature is wonderful in all seasons and the changes they bring.

Weeping Willows
These willows seem to have wept enough to create a mini-mangrove swamp around
their feet, near the children's playground on Wellingborough's Embankment area.

Riverside Park
Spring sunshine was around but this deep frost pocket kept the ground frozen despite the rising air temperature.

Green Logs
Folk lore stories abound with references to "the Green Man"… looking at this pile of moss-covered logs it is easy to see where the stories started amongst our forest-dwelling ancestors.

Fishing Platform
No chance of a catch today, but the cracking ice tells the story that winter is loosening its grip on
the water around this fishing platform at Higham Ferrers' Riverside Country Park.

Opposite:
Higham Ferrers' Swans
These swans have been nesting here for several years and the sunshine has tempted them to check out their nest site at the Riverside Park
outside Higham Ferrers. They will be here sitting on eggs in May, but for the moment the cob seems especially pleased with himself!

Sulgrave Stocks
The old stocks at Sulgrave could probably tell some interesting stories,
but the spring crocus captured my eye on a bright March afternoon.

Sulgrave Manor
This slightly surreal scene is at Sulgrave Manor, where a guide in traditional
Elizabethan dress takes a break from his duties in re-enactment of life at Sulgrave
in the sixteenth century. The statue of course is of George Washington, the first
President of the United States, and Sulgrave was the home of his ancestors
before their departure for Virginia in 1656. In 1914 the house was presented to
the nation by a group of British donors to commemorate the Hundred Years
Peace between the two nations. In 1924, the National Society of Colonial Dames
of America generously endowed the Manor House and still co-operates in
its upkeep. The Manor stands as a permanent reminder of the special relationship
between Britain and America, and today visitors from all over the world,
including many school children, come to enjoy this beautiful Tudor house.

Canons Ashby Gardens

Work on the formal gardens must continue thoughout the winter to ensure a stunning spring display at the lovely Elizabethan mansion. The topiary and lawns were getting special attention after the heavy snow in January. Canons Ashby is a romantic, Elizabethan house, which has survived unaltered since 1710. Home of the Dryden family since it was first built, the gardens are an especially nice feature. The park and gardens contain lawns, herbaceous borders, topiary, shrubs, trees, an orchard and a wild flower meadow.

Canons Ashby Church
The Priory Church of St Mary is all that now remains of the twelfth century Augustinian priory from which Canons Ashby takes its name.
On an otherwise overcast March day, sun lights up the church.

Thaw
As the snow releases its grip on the land, reviving warmth gets through the leaf mould and bark to warm the soil.

Salcey Catkins
Deep in Salcey Forest these catkins dance in the breeze as February's freeze turns into a mild March morning.

Castle Ashby Cricket Pavilion
Although never likely to be used again, this ancient cricket pavilion at Castle Ashby reminds us that the summer will be back with days sitting watching a game under the shade of a tree. The cricket pitch at Castle Ashby enjoys a setting that many village clubs would envy… right in view of the great house.

A walk by the canal
Spring is here and the towpath at Stoke Bruerne is a great place for a brisk walk in the sunshine – coats off, the sun is back!